Easter Bunnies

By Stephen Cosgrove
Illustrated by Wendy Edelson

IDEALS CHILDREN'S BOOKS
Nashville, Tennessee

4/72

Published by Ideals Publishing Corporation
Nelson Place at Elm Hill Pike
Nashville, Tennessee 37214
ISBN 0-8249-8318-1

Dedicated to the Franchimones—Sam, Tina, Dana, and John Michael.
They taught me to give. . . from the heart.

Stephen

Beyond tomorrow in the middle
of April or May,
Winter sneezed a sneeze and then
just went away.
Springtime took over in leaps and
in bounds,
Waving spring flowers that had
bloomed all around.

The creatures of the meadow sniffed,
stretched, and yawned.
"Yea and hooray!" they shouted.
"Winter is gone."
The meadow was filled with
excitement that day
As the warm springtime breezes
blew winter away.

Living in this meadow, in a cottage
   bright and sunny,
There lived a big family—simply
   called the Boo Bunnies.
There were Momma and Poppa and,
   of course, babies too.
There were four or five babies, which
   is a lot more than two.

The first day of spring excitement
   sprung loose—
Yes, in the Boo cottage like a long-
   legged goose.
Momma scolded the children, "For
   pity's sake!"
As Poppa whipped up a breakfast
   of peach porridge and cake.

The smallest of the bunnies was
   called Peeka Boo,
And he was hungrier than hungry.
   He needed some food!
He had just come to breakfast from
   his nighttime snooze
In hand-me-down pajamas and
   hand-me-down shoes.

(Being the smallest can really be a
   scare
If no older Boo Bunny will boost you
   up in your chair.)

When breakfast was done, Poppa
    Boo laughed in glee,
"It's time for spring cleaning." The
    bunnies groaned, "Oh, gee!"
For springtime to children means
    playing outside.
But cleaning the house. . . that they
    couldn't abide.

Chairs scraped and screeched on the
    old, wooden floor
As all the Boo Bunnies slipped right
    out the door.
Poppa Boo was shocked and Momma
    was too.
They were left all alone. Oh yes, it
    was true.

Momma and Poppa whisked, dusted,
  and cleaned
Inside and outside their home, so it
  seemed.
They cleaned the curtains and the
  old, shuttered blinds.
Both inside and out, the windows
  they shined.

But all over the house, under the
  ruffles too,
The children were hidden. . . little
  bunnies Boo.

When all was done, they sat with a thump
In an overstuffed chair made from an old
   cedar stump.
There, cuddled together, they fell fast
   asleep,
As little Boo Bunnies from their hiding
   did creep.

"They're all worn out!" the Boo Bunnies
   cried.
"We should have helped them or at least
   should have tried."
Tears dripped and dropped from fuzzy,
   young cheeks
Like raindrops from heaven. . . soon a river,
   a creek.

Little baby Boo Bunnies felt so
    very bad;
Even little Peeka Boo was terri-
    bly sad.
"I know," said the oldest, as he
    snuffled and sniffed,
"We should buy them a present. . .
    a token, a gift."

"What a great idea," the Boo
    Bunnies agreed,
"To say that we are sorry for our
    awful deed."
With muffled feet and *Shhh*'s all
    around,
They sneaked outside and then
    rushed into town.

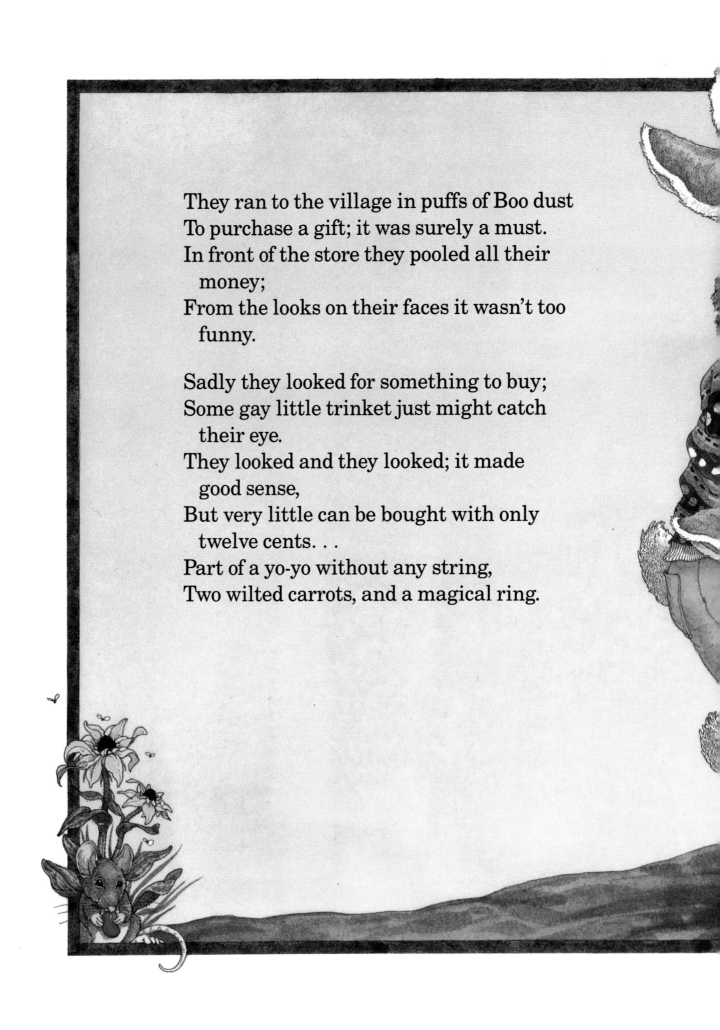

They ran to the village in puffs of Boo dust
To purchase a gift; it was surely a must.
In front of the store they pooled all their
    money;
From the looks on their faces it wasn't too
    funny.

Sadly they looked for something to buy;
Some gay little trinket just might catch
    their eye.
They looked and they looked; it made
    good sense,
But very little can be bought with only
    twelve cents. . .
Part of a yo-yo without any string,
Two wilted carrots, and a magical ring.

They bought weaving straw, some
  bright, golden twine,
A bit of silk ribbon—all would do
  just fine,
For a basket they'd weave, and a
  basket they'd make.
But what to put in it? "Oh, for
  pity's sake!"

They had spent all their money
  except for a penny.
Not much would that buy—not
  much, if any.
But there was an eggshell sitting
  high on the shelf,
And for only one cent, just help
  yourself.

It was monstrously big and broken
  in two,
But Boo Bunnies were smart; they
  knew what to do!

They rushed back to Boo cottage, and
hiding behind,
They wove straw and ribbon with flowers
and vine.
They wove and they wove for an hour or
more;
Little Peeka fell asleep in the middle of
their chore.

But no matter to Boo Bunnies if the baby
did sleep,
They just rolled him aside into the straw
so deep.
They worked and they worked as they sang
"Tisket-a-tasket."
And they wove and they twined a beautiful
basket.

When the basket was done, they
  took the eggshell,
And with pitch from the pine they
  glued it so well.
Then to be certain that it stayed
  firm and fine,
They wrapped it thrice over with
  bright, golden twine.

When the glue was dry and the
  twine tied just so,
They painted that egg so the cracks
  wouldn't show.
They painted and painted the
  bottom and sides
All the colors of the rainbow for no
  Boo could decide.

Oh, it was many colors, that egg in
  the shade,
And the bunnies were proud of the
  gift they had made.

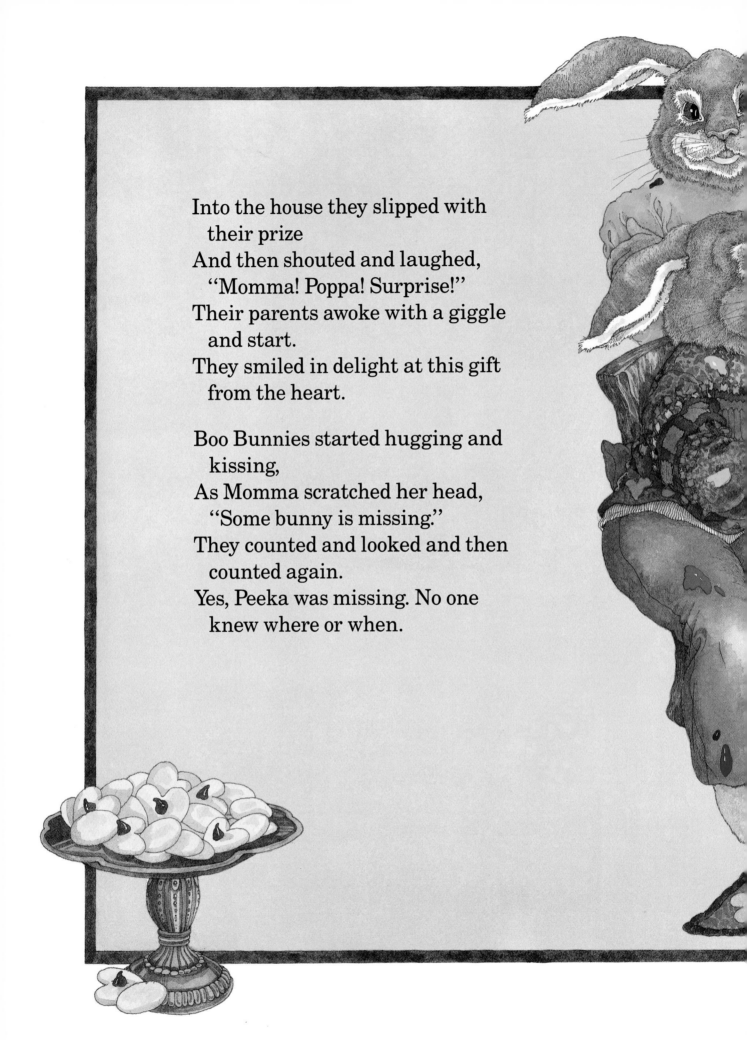

Into the house they slipped with
    their prize
And then shouted and laughed,
    "Momma! Poppa! Surprise!"
Their parents awoke with a giggle
    and start.
They smiled in delight at this gift
    from the heart.

Boo Bunnies started hugging and
    kissing,
As Momma scratched her head,
    "Some bunny is missing."
They counted and looked and then
    counted again.
Yes, Peeka was missing. No one
    knew where or when.

Suddenly, the egg wiggle-squiggled
  and cracked.
There he was in the shell, as a
  matter of fact.
His fur was all colored an eggshell
  blue.
He felt sort of silly as Momma
  laughed, "Peeka Boo!"

Boo Bunnies are loved every day in
  the spring
For love from the heart is the gift
  that they bring.

About the Author

In 1973 Stephen Cosgrove stumbled into a bookstore to buy a fantasy book for his daughter but couldn't find one that he really liked. He decided he was looking for something that hadn't been written. "I went home and that night I wrote my first book."

Since that fledgling effort over a decade ago, Cosgrove's books have sold millions of copies worldwide.

Cosgrove was born in 1945. He attended Stephens College for Women in Columbia, Missouri ("A great year but I learned little and forgot a lot"), is married, and lives on a quiet, little farm in Washington. There he writes on his computer, communicates by telefax with eight children's book illustrators about current projects, and takes healthy breaks to play with the dog and pick the daisies.

Other books by Stephen Cosgrove

Favorite Fairy Tales
Billy Goats Gruff
Goldilocks
Humpity Dumpity
Three Blind Mice

Simple Folk
Chores
Kind and Gentle Ladies
Nosey Birds
The Picnic

Hippity Hoppity
Flippity Floppity